YEAR 3

WRITING

2011 edition including persuasive writing

NAPLAN*-FORMAT PRACTICE TESTS
with answers

Essential preparation for Year 3
NAPLAN* Tests Writing

Alfred Fletcher

CORONEOS PUBLICATIONS

YEAR 3 WRITING
NAPLAN*- FORMAT PRACTICE TESTS with answers
© Alfred Fletcher 2011
Published by Coroneos Publications 2011

ISBN 978-1-921565-91-5

* These tests have been produced by Coroneos Publications independently of Australian governments and are not officially endorsed publications of the NAPLAN program.

THIS BOOK IS AVAILABLE FROM RECOGNISED BOOKSELLERS OR CONTACT:

Coroneos Publications
Telephone: (02) 9624 3977   Facsimile: (02) 9624 3717
Business Address: 6/195 Prospect Highway Seven Hills 2147
Postal Address: PO Box 2 Seven Hills 2147
Website: www.coroneos.com.au or www.basicskillsseries.com
E-mail: coroneospublications@westnet.com.au

Contents

Introductory Notes and the NAPLAN* Test. . . . .Page 4

Writing Persuasive Texts (7 Tests). . . . . .Page 12

Writing Descriptions (3 Tests). . . . . .Page 38

Writing Recounts (3 Tests). . . . . .Page 48

Writing Information Reports (3 Tests). . . . . . . .Page 58

Writing Narrative (3 Tests). . . . . .Page 68

Model Answers to all Questions. . . . . .Page 78

NOTE:
- Students have 40 minutes to complete a test.
- Students must use 2B or HB pencils only.

Introductory Notes and the NAPLAN* Test

This book is designed to help you practise for the Writing section of the NAPLAN* test and develop the skills necessary to competently handle any writing task presented to you at this stage of your development. To date the NAPLAN* writing test has been a narrative but now has changed to persuasive writing. Here we have included examples of other types of writing you will experience during your schooling. Practising these will develop skills that will assist you in all areas of your writing.

Also included in this book are some hints on how to improve your writing. Follow these hints and use them in your work as they may assist you in gaining additional vital marks under examination conditions. They will also help you develop your vocabulary which is vital to good, concise and clear writing. We wish you all the best for the exam and know that the activities and tasks in this book will assist you in reaching your writing potential.

* These tests have been produced by Coroneos Publications independently of Australian governments and are not officially endorsed publications of the NAPLAN program

The Writing Task

The NAPLAN* test includes a writing task which is now a persuasive text. Persuasive writing is basically a way of arguing or discussing an idea. You could agree or disagree or argue both points of view. A persuasive text allows you to give your opinion on an idea or topic and use evidence and clear reasons why your ideas are correct. One of the main things to remember is that you still have to write clearly and attempt to convince the reader that your opinions are correct.

Typical topics for a persuasive writing task could be...

- Junk food should be banned.
- Australia's flag should be changed.
- Branded clothing should be banned.

When you consider topics such as these, it is possible to support or argue against the the idea suggested by the topic. In writing the piece you are expected to examine both sides of the question, balancing the competing ideas before coming to a conclusion.

A stimulus text on the topic will be provided: this may be images [pictures] or words or both. You can use these ideas in your writing or you can just use your own ideas. The choice is yours and you should decide this reasonably quickly so you can begin to write. You won't lose marks for using your own ideas. Pay attention to all the instructions and use your planning time well. The instructions on the test may tell you to think about the characters you will use, the complication or problem and the end. It will also tell you to write in sentences, pay attention to vocabulary, spelling and punctuation. An instruction may also be that your work may be published so that you need to edit carefully.

The time allowed for the test will be

- five (5) minutes of planning time
- thirty (30) minutes to write the text.
- five (5) minutes to edit your work.

The editing process is important and you should use this time to check your work including spelling and punctuation. One easy structural thing to check is paragraphs. Look at your work to see if you have forgotten to use them in your rush to write your piece.

What Markers Look For When Examining Your Work

When examiners mark your work they have some specific guidelines. Currently there are ten (10) criteria that are used for marking the writing task. These are shown below and a mark or score range is used for each one.

- ☑ Audience
- ☑ Text structure
- ☑ Ideas
- ☑ Persuasive Devices
- ☑ Vocabulary
- ☑ Cohesion
- ☑ Paragraphing
- ☑ Sentence structure
- ☑ Punctuation
- ☑ Spelling

Most of these terms are self explanatory but the term cohesion just means that your story holds together with one idea or line of thought. As you get older you will see the term 'sustained writing' which means much the same thing. By understanding clearly the information you have just read you will have taken the first major step on your path to success in these tests. By knowing what you have to do you will be prepared for it and confident in what you need to do to succeed. Re-read these introductory notes several times. Then you know what to expect in the exam and won't be surprised by the words in the exam or the format. The next section gives you some writing tips to help improve your writing.

Improving Your Writing

Writing improvement is a matter of practice and developing your skills and vocabulary so you can express yourself clearly.

Writing in the Correct Text Type

When you are asked to write in a particular text type make sure that you follow the correct structure or format for that type of writing. For example in a narrative you would use the structure: orientation, complication and resolution. In persuasive writing you would make an argument for a particular viewpoint using persuasive language. Try to know all the different types and what is required. This book will help you to do that.

Ensuring Cohesion

To ensure that your story sticks together it is best to have one idea that holds the story together. If you have too many ideas your story will become confused and so will your readers or audience. Remember to stick to the topic or idea you are given in the stimulus material for the exam. Make sure the tense of the story is consistent and you have sustained the main idea.

Write in Paragraphs

One of the marking criterias for the exam is paragraphing and you should begin a new paragraph for a new thought or concept in your story. Shorter paragraphs are usually clearer and audiences like to be clear on what they are reading. If you get to the end of your story and begin to edit and notice you don't have paragraphs you can still put them in. To do this you can just put a [symbol before the word where a new paragraph starts. The marker will understand what you mean.

Engaging the Audience

To engage and entertain an audience a good introduction is necessary. It needs to be interesting and make the audience want to read on. You can practise this by writing different introductions to the same story and seeing which one your family and friends like best. The same idea is also relevant to the resolution. Audiences don't like stories which don't have an ending that solves the puzzle or complication in the story. Use the planning time to work out your ending.

Vocabulary

Vocabulary is a powerful tool for the writer to have. Word choices help expression and make your idea(s) easy for the audience to understand. To improve your vocabulary you can use a dictionary and a thesaurus to find new words. Make sure you understand what a word means before you use it and also how to use it correctly. Don't just use 'big' words to impress.

Sentence Structure

When you write your work make sure you write in sentences. As you learn to write you will use longer or compound sentences. Sentences should begin with a capital letter and end with a piece of punctuation such as a full stop or question mark. This will help the marker know you can use a sentence.

Spelling

Spelling is something that can be practised if you are not as strong in this area as you might be. Word lists can be useful and there are many good spelling books that can assist you in developing your skills. Don't be afraid to use new words as you can correct spelling in the editing process.

Editing

The editing process is an important one and you have five (5) minutes at the end of the test to edit. In your mind you should have a mental list of the areas the examiners are looking for and work on those. Think of things like tense and ask yourself whether your persuasive text has the correct structure. Re-read your work and fix little errors in the spelling, punctuation and grammar that may occur under exam conditions.

Writing A Persuasive Text

The planning time before you begin writing will help you decide on your idea and plan how you will maintain it. You only have thirty minutes to write so don't plan for too many arguments and think about your concluding paragraph so you don't have to rush final paragraphs and spoil your argument.

Other Types Of Writing

Information Reports

These present facts and information. Here you can use sub-headings for different sections. You need to use clear, concise sentences under these sub headings.

Recounts

A recount remembers or recalls events that have already happened. You will need to write these events in the time or chronological order in which they occurred but you can include some personal thoughts on the event. Usually an orientation tells the reader who, where and when.

Descriptions

A description gives details about the five senses (touch, taste, sight, sound and smell) but can also include emotions and/or feelings if necessary. You still need to orientate the reader in your description.

Narratives

The basic structure of a narrative is orientation [introduction], complication [problem], resolution [conclusion]. Each of these MUST be included in your narrative or story. It is particularly important to have a strong introduction and resolution to leave your audience satisfied at the end of their reading.

In clarifying your thoughts on the structure an orientation tells the audience the WHO, WHERE and WHEN of the story while the complication is the problem that arises in the narrative. The resolution or conclusion to your story needs to have a solution to the complication you have created. A complication to our story might be an unexpected storm that traps Sybil and the resolution might be her rescue by helicopter. The complication usually leads to the climax or most exciting part of the story. It is important to focus on one main idea or theme in the story so as to remain consistent throughout the narrative. This will stop you and the audience becoming confused about a number of ideas.

You are about to write a persuasive text. The topic for your writing is:

Convince someone to take you to the beach.

What do you feel about this idea? Write to show your opinions to a reader.

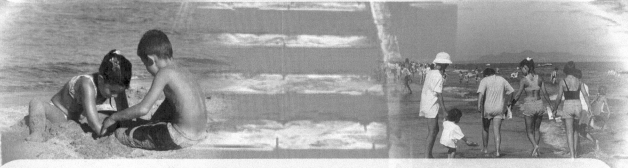

Think about:
- If you can see both sides of the argument or just one
- A clear introduction that gives your ideas on the topic
- Opinions with evidence and explanation
- The conclusion where you give a summary of your ideas

Remember to:
- Make a plan
- Use sentences
- Think about punctuation and spelling
- Make sensible word choices that show the reader your opinions
- Use paragraphs
- Edit your writing and check carefully so your work is clear.

1. Convince someone to take you to the beach.

State whether you agree, disagree or see both sides of the argument.

Be clear with your ideas.

The beach is the best place to take small children, family, relatives and friends. At the beach there are many things to do, games to play, healthy activities and swimming. The adults can just lie on the beach and relax or get a chair under the umbrella and pass the time in any way they wish. Finally the beach is free which is great for budgeting families. We just have to go!

Try and have an interesting concluding sentence in the introduction to capture the reader's attention.

Persuasive language can be emotive e.g. fabulous or you can ask questions.

Firstly at the beach there are many fabulous things to do such as building sandcastles, collecting shells, jumping waves and splashing about. These are all healthy activities that have you out in the fresh air. At the beach you can have fun and get fit at the same time. What more could you ask for?

Try and interest the reader by including reasons and evidence to support your ideas.

Secondly the beach is a great place to go for all ages and types of people. While the children are out romping the adults can lie around and relax, perhaps reading a book or magazine or just listening to music. More mature people can grab a chair and stay out of the sun while still benefiting from the healthy atmosphere. What a great way to spend the day. A cool drink while the afternoon breeze comes in off the ocean. Fantastic.

Clear logical sequence to the arguments.

Give examples to support your argument.

Finally the beach is a wonderful place to go and it is free. There are not many places you can go and have this much fun for everyone without paying a fortune. The only cost at the beach would be the ice-cream that you buy me on the way home. How good is that?

In conclusion we should go to the beach because it offers something for everyone and there is no better place to go for fun.

A strong conclusion is needed that restates or summarises your main points again. This reinforces your ideas.

You are about to write a persuasive text. The topic for your writing is:

It is better to be an only child.
What do you feel about this idea? Write to show your opinions to a reader.

ONLY CHILD

Think about:
- If you can see both sides of the argument or just one
- A clear introduction that gives your ideas on the topic
- Opinions with evidence and explanation
- The conclusion where you give a summary of your ideas

Remember to:
- Make a plan
- Use sentences
- Think about punctuation and spelling
- Make sensible word choices that show the reader your opinions
- Use paragraphs
- Edit your writing and check carefully so your work is clear.

2. It is better to be an only child

....

....

....

....

....

....

....

....

....

....

....

....

....

....

....

....

You are about to write a persuasive text. The topic for your writing is:

Riding bikes on the road is dangerous.
What do you feel about this idea? Write to show your opinions to a reader.

Think about:
- If you can see both sides of the argument or just one
- A clear introduction that gives your ideas on the topic
- Opinions with evidence and explanation
- The conclusion where you give a summary of your ideas

Remember to:
- Make a plan
- Use sentences
- Think about punctuation and spelling
- Make sensible word choices that show the reader your opinions
- Use paragraphs
- Edit your writing and check carefully so your work is clear.

3. Riding Bikes on the road is dangerous.

You are about to write a persuasive text. The topic for your writing is:

Board games are better than video games.

What do you feel about this idea? Write to show your opinions to a reader.

BOARD GAMES

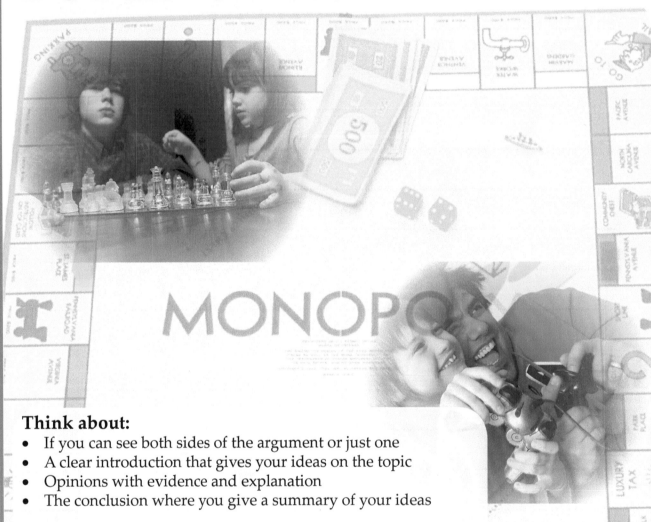

Think about:
- If you can see both sides of the argument or just one
- A clear introduction that gives your ideas on the topic
- Opinions with evidence and explanation
- The conclusion where you give a summary of your ideas

Remember to:
- Make a plan
- Use sentences
- Think about punctuation and spelling
- Make sensible word choices that show the reader your opinions
- Use paragraphs
- Edit your writing and check carefully so your work is clear.

4. Board games are better than video games.

....

....

....

....

....

....

....

....

....

....

....

....

....

....

....

....

© Alfred Fletcher
Coroneos Publications

© Alfred Fletcher
Coroneos Publications

Year 3 Writing
NAPLAN*-Format Practice Tests

You are about to write a persuasive text. The topic for your writing is:

It is better to grow vegetables than flowers.

What do you feel about this idea? Write to show your opinions to a reader

VEGETABLES

Think about:
- If you can see both sides of the argument or just one
- A clear introduction that gives your ideas on the topic
- Opinions with evidence and explanation
- The conclusion where you give a summary of your ideas

Remember to:
- Make a plan
- Use sentences
- Think about punctuation and spelling
- Make sensible word choices that show the reader your opinions
- Use paragraphs
- Edit your writing and check carefully so your work is clear.

5. It is better to grow vegetables than flowers.

....

....

....

....

....

....

....

....

....

....

....

....

....

....

....

....

....

....

....

....

....

....

....

....

....

....

....

....

....

....

....

....

....

....

....

You are about to write a persuasive text. The topic for your writing is:

Schools should make lunchtime longer.

What do you feel about this idea? Write to show your opinions to a reader.

Think about:
- If you can see both sides of the argument or just one
- A clear introduction that gives your ideas on the topic
- Opinions with evidence and explanation
- The conclusion where you give a summary of your ideas

Remember to:
- Make a plan
- Use sentences
- Think about punctuation and spelling
- Make sensible word choices that show the reader your opinions
- Use paragraphs
- Edit your writing and check carefully so your work is clear.

6. School should make lunchtime longer.

© Alfred Fletcher
Coroneos Publications

You are about to write a persuasive text. The topic for your writing is:

Persuade an adult to buy something you really want.

What do you feel about this idea? Write to show your opinions to a reader.

Think about:
- If you can see both sides of the argument or just one
- A clear introduction that gives your ideas on the topic
- Opinions with evidence and explanation
- The conclusion where you give a summary of your ideas

Remember to:
- Make a plan
- Use sentences
- Think about punctuation and spelling
- Make sensible word choices that show the reader your opinions
- Use paragraphs
- Edit your writing and check carefully so your work is clear.

7. Persuade an adult to buy something you really want.

....

....

....

....

....

....

....

....

....

....

....

....

....

....

....

....

....

....

Gardens can be large or small, be created in cities or the countryside. You may have a garden of your own with flowers, trees or even vegetables.

Write a description of a garden you know or create one in your imagination

8. Garden

Introduction

Tells what is being described, why and when. Sets the scene.

My garden is large enough for us to have plenty of grassy space to play hide and seek, soccer and cricket. My mother and father have lots of flower gardens which they spend time in each weekend while my sister and two brothers play.

Body

Gives description of what the writer experiences. Use sight, sound, smell, taste and touch

The gardens are filled with flowers of every imaginable colour. In spring you can see the blues, reds, yellows, pinks and whites from the road. People who walk past tell my parents they can smell the fragrance from the different plants as you walk past. The flowers are in many shapes and sizes but my favourites are the purple pansies and the bright blue cornflowers.

The front garden also has a hedge to stop people seeing in all the way. The plant in the hedge is called plumbago and it has blue and white flowers and is always green even in winter. This hedge is clipped back with big cutters each year or else it would get too high. Dad says it needs to be kept tidy and under control.

My favourite place in the garden is the old mulberry tree in the backyard. It is about ten times taller than me and the thick, brown branches are good for climbing. The leaves are soft so they don't scratch you and each year it has fruit on it which are purple and taste delicious. The mulberry juice stains your teeth and tongue. Sometimes it even stains your clothes.

Conclusion

Does not have to end like a narrative but you need to indicate that the description is complete.

My garden is a safe and pleasant place to play and on Sundays we might have a barbecue for lunch and sit at the outside table to eat. That's always fun.

Games are many and vary greatly in rules or where they are played. Games can be played by yourself, in pairs or in a team.

Write a description of a game you have played or seen someone play.

GAME

9. Game

....

....

....

....

....

....

....

....

....

....

....

....

....

....

....

....

....

....

© Alfred Fletcher
Coroneos Publications

....

....

....

....

....

....

....

....

....

....

....

....

....

....

....

....

....

HORSES

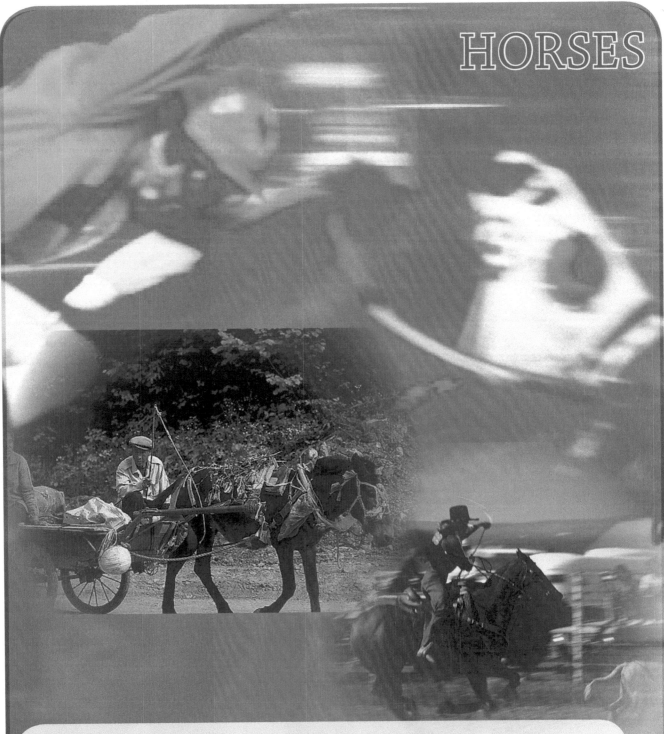

Horses come in many sizes and colours. They can be used to ride, pull wagons, race or muster sheep and cattle in the bush.

Write a description of a horse you have seen in a picture or in real life.

10. Horses

© Alfred Fletcher
Coroneos Publications

BEST
BIRTHDAY

Write a recount of your best birthday

11. Best Birthday

Introduction

Sets the scene for what is happening and tells time and place etc

My best birthday was the birthday party I had when I was eight. It had everything that a fantastic birthday should have; friends, family, presents and a wonderful time. Let me tell you about it.

When I woke up in the morning we had a family gathering and I received the presents my family had bought me. I had a new computer, an MP3 player, and some games for the Playstation and clothing. What a fabulous start to the day. Then mum made pancakes for breakfast which we all enjoyed thoroughly.

Body

Tells what is happening in chronological order with some personal comments

We then got ready and went to my grandparent's place where we had morning tea. They gave me some games for the new computer which was really nice of them. On the way home mum and dad bought all the things we needed for the afternoon. I got to choose the foods that my friends and I would eat.

At three o'clock my three best friends came over and to top it off a big truck arrived with a jumping castle. We stayed on it all afternoon long before becoming very tired of jumping. As it was a sleepover my friends stayed for tea and we ate pizza and all the yummy lollies we bought earlier in the day.

Conclusion

Finishes the recount and ends the event or what happened. Can have personal comment

My friends and I stayed up very late and watched a scary movie. We then stayed in our sleeping bags and talked and told jokes until nearly midnight. We soon fell asleep because we were so tired. We woke the next morning very early and continued to talk. My friends had a great time. What a birthday!

Write a recount of your worst holiday

WORST HOLIDAY

12. Worst Holiday

Write a recount of an accident you have had or seen.

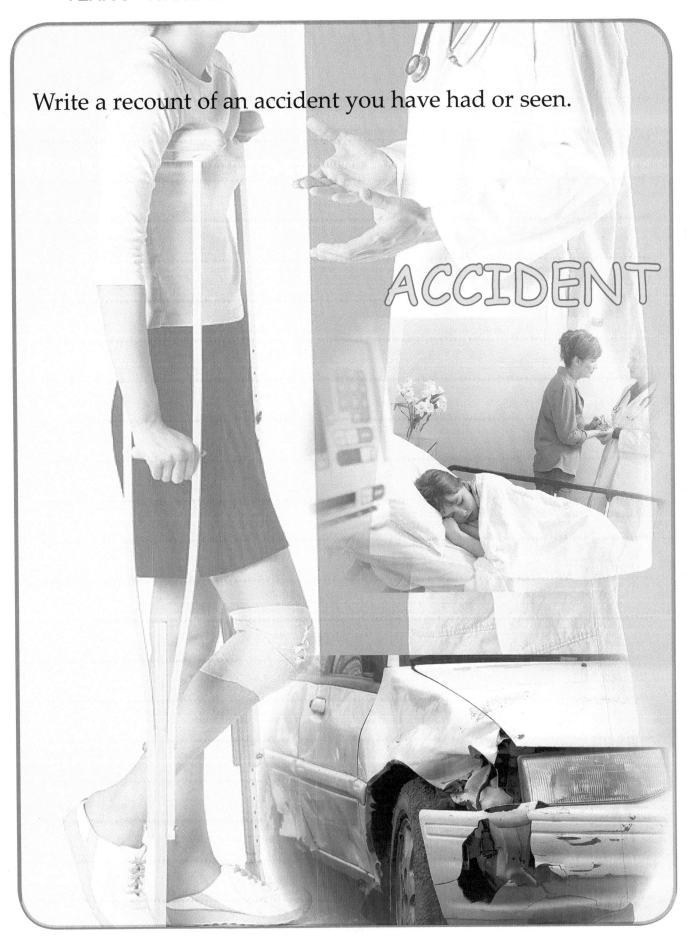

ACCIDENT

© Alfred Fletcher
Coroneos Publications

13. Accident

....

....

....

....

....

....

....

....

....

....

....

....

....

....

....

....

....

© Alfred Fletcher
Coroneos Publications

Year 3 Writing
NAPLAN*-Format Practice Tests

Compile a report about dinosaurs. You may wish to report on the different types of dinosaurs, how they lived, what they ate, how they became extinct and any other ideas that you have about the topic.

14. Dinosaurs

Introduction

Gives a general overview of the topic and some information.

What are dinosaurs?

Dinosaurs were a large group of very different animals many millions of years ago. They are mainly reptiles and birds with more than one thousand five hundred species. The word dinosaur was given by a British scientist Richard Owen and it means 'terrible, powerful, wondrous lizard'.

Sections with sub-headings

Each section has a sub-heading which alerts the reader to the topic. Language is factual not emotional.

What did dinosaurs eat?

Dinosaurs ate both plants and animals. This means some were carnivores (meat eating) and some were herbivores (plant eating). Some dinosaurs ate both plants and animals which means they were omnivores.

What happened to the dinosaurs?

There are no true dinosaurs left on earth and they became extinct. Other types of animals on earth also became extinct at this time and scientists think a meteor hit the earth and changed the atmosphere. There are some other theories about the extinction and one is that the dinosaurs just failed to adapt to a changing world environment.

Conclusion

May give some conclusions or general ideas about the topic.

How do we know about dinosaurs?

We know about dinosaurs through fossils of dinosaur bones that scientists have dug up from the ground. They find bones and then reassemble them to show what the animal looked like. You can see dinosaur bones in museums.

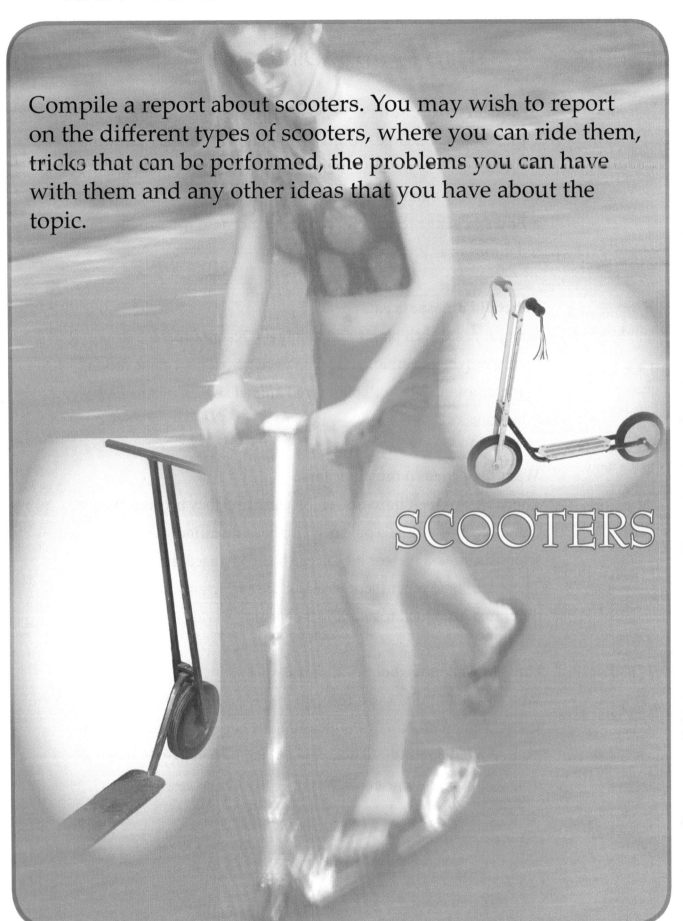

Compile a report about scooters. You may wish to report on the different types of scooters, where you can ride them, tricks that can be performed, the problems you can have with them and any other ideas that you have about the topic.

SCOOTERS

15. Scooters

....

....

....

....

....

....

....

....

....

....

....

....

....

....

....

....

....

Compile a report about bread. You may wish to report on the different types of breads, how they bake bread, the ingredients of bread, why bread is good for you and any other ideas that you have about the topic.

© Alfred Fletcher
Coroneos Publications

16. Bread

....

....

....

....

....

....

....

....

....

....

....

....

....

....

....

....

....

You are about to write a story or narrative. The topic for your work is treasure. Treasure can be found in many places and doesn't have to be gold or jewels it could be magical or a person. Some words to help you with your story are: map, friendship and discover.

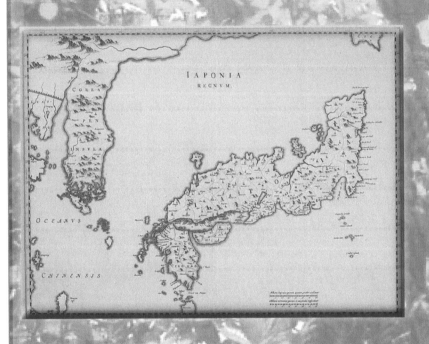

TREASURE

17. Treasure

Orientation
or introduction
has the who,
when and
where of the
story and a
hint at the
complication.

Tells what
is being
described, why
and when. Sets
the scene.

The desert was so hot. The sand went on forever and each step was very difficult. I didn't think that my friends and I would make it out alive. We had been lost when our little plane crashed on our way to my parents' worksite at the pyramids. The pilot was injured badly so we went for help. So far we'd found nothing and Sally looked very sunburnt and tired. Nathaniel was dragging his leg which had been wrenched in the crash.

I didn't feel all that well myself and with the water running out things were not looking positive. If we didn't find someone or something soon we would not be able to save ourselves, let alone the pilot. I adjusted my hat and pushed ahead.

Complication

The problem
of the story.
Usually comes to
a climax before
problem is
solved

'I think were not gonna make it,' said Nathaniel. 'It is too hot to survive out here.'

'Be positive,' I replied smiling at Sally. 'We'll be fine we just have to keep going.'

The three of us continued to walk in silence. Sand dune after sand dune we climbed. I was beginning to feel that we were in big trouble when in the distance I saw what looked like an oasis. I shouted with joy but Sally warned it might be a mirage.

Resolution

The ending.
Here the story
has a happy
ending but the
resolution does
not have to be
happy

We ran toward it and it was real! Inside the shade of the palm trees was a small well made by the local tribesmen. The water inside was better than any treasure we could have found. Refreshed and cool we knew someone would come here soon and we were saved.

You are about to write a story or narrative. The topic for your work is lost. Many things can be lost such as keys, pets, books but also harder things like people and time. Some words to help you with your story are: luckily, saddened and search.

18. Lost

© Alfred Fletcher
Coroneos Publications

Year 3 Writing
NAPLAN*-Format Practice Tests

You are about to write a story or narrative. The topic for your work is island. Islands can have resorts for holidays or be large like Australia. You could be shipwrecked on one. Some words to help you with your story are: sandy, huts and people.

ISLAND

19. Island

....

....

....

....

....

....

....

....

....

....

....

....

....

....

....

....

....

Sample Responses - Persuasive Writing

1. Convince someone to take you to the beach

The beach is the best place to take small children, family, relatives and friends. At the beach there are many things to do, games to play, healthy activities and swimming. The adults can just lie on the beach and relax or get a chair under the umbrella and pass the time in any way they wish. Finally the beach is free which is great for budgeting families. We just have to go!

Firstly at the beach there are many fabulous things to do such as building sandcastles, collecting shells, jumping waves and splashing about. These are all healthy activities that have you out in the fresh air. At the beach you can have fun and get fit at the same time. What more could you ask for?

Secondly the beach is a great place to go for all ages and types of people. While the children are out romping the adults can lie around and relax, perhaps reading a book or magazine or just listening to music. More mature people can grab a chair and stay out of the sun while still benefiting from the healthy atmosphere. What a great way to spend the day. A cool drink while the afternoon breeze comes in off the ocean. Fantastic.

Finally the beach is a wonderful place to go and it is free. There are not many places you can go and have this much fun for everyone without paying a fortune. The only cost at the beach would be the ice-cream that you buy me on the way home. How good is that?

In conclusion we should go to the beach because it offers something for everyone and there is no better place to go for fun.

2. It is better to be an only child

It is not better to be an only child. The only child can grow up lonely without any brothers and sisters to have fun with. Only children can also grow up to be spoilt and this makes them selfish. The final reason that it is not better to be an only child is that when you are older you have nobody to share special days with like large families do. It is undoubtedly better to come from a family with siblings.

As an only child you have no one in the home to share games with, watch television with or just hang about talking. If your parents are out you are totally alone and can be very bored and lonely. Children with brothers and sisters can play games, chat and generally muck about. It is boring doing this on your own.

Children who grow up as the only child can become very spoilt and selfish. They do not have to share their toys, their parents have no choice but to give them everything and they get all the attention. This can lead to them being selfish teenagers and generate other social problems. Being an only child does have its drawbacks.

Another reason it is not good to be an only child is that when you are older those special days that are shared by large families don't happen. You can be there all by yourself with no one to celebrate with. This is very sad and would make you unhappy. It is much better to have a large family where you all get together and have heaps of fun. These occasions are to be remembered. Bad luck if you're on your own.

It is far better to have siblings than to be an only child for the reasons outlined.

3. Riding bikes on the road is dangerous

Riding bikes on the road is extremely dangerous and should be avoided at all times. On a bike you are extremely vulnerable to trucks and other large vehicles with poor vision of children on bikes. Another reason to stay off the road is that they are designed for cars and not for bikes. The two do not mix. The final reason that riding bikes on the road is dangerous is that children are not taught the road rules at an early age and this leaves them unaware of things they may be doing wrong which can get them in trouble.

Staying off the road is the sensible thing to do. Large trucks and other dangerous vehicles find it hard to see little children on bikes. This leaves you vulnerable to an accident. These days trucks are so big that they might not even notice hitting you. It is so easy to be injured or even killed. Stay off the road at all costs.

Roads are designed for cars and this is a good reason to not ride your bike on the road. Many roads are too narrow for cars and bikes. In this case the cars win every time. You could be placing your life in danger just by being on the road. It is much safer to ride on the footpath with your helmet on. Other places to ride instead of the road might be bush trails, parks and ovals.

The final reason to stay off the road is that young children have not been taught the road rules or any of the signals necessary to alert drivers to what you are doing. This can lead to accidents which are dangerous for all road users.

Have no doubt it is extremely dangerous to ride bikes on the road.

4. Board games are better than video games

Board games are much better than video games for several very good reasons. Board games are far more interactive and thought provoking than the mundane video games that turn individuals into drones. Board games also help people socially as you have to communicate with others during a board game. Computers make people lonely as you play a machine alone. Board games are also able to be played anywhere without complicated machinery or internet connections.

Board games are so varied that you could not describe them all. From Monopoly to chess through to Scrabble they are always varied and entertaining. You develop many wonderful skills when playing board games and grow your intellect. Poor old video games are basically shoot 'em and smash 'em up type games that are entertaining for a short time but don't extend or stretch the mind.

Board games are also great for large gatherings where six people can play the same game at the same time. They encourage co-operation and interaction. This is not so for the video game which at most requires two players and more often one. This does not encourage social interaction and makes for solitary people. So board games are much better in this respect.

My final argument is that board games are easier to play in difficult locations or where you have no computers such as when you are on holidays. They are a whole heap of fun in a box. This is not so for video games which require complicated electronic equipment that is prone to failure.

In conclusion it is safe to say that board games are definitely better than video games.

5. It is better to grow vegetables than flowers

It certainly is better to grow vegetables rather than flowers for the reasons outlined below. Vegetables are useful while flowers are only for decoration. Vegetables can be used for many things and in many ways while flowers are single purpose albeit beautiful items. Vegetables can also produce income in hard times and can be traded or bartered whereas flowers are not so essential to life. When you consider the issue it is certainly better to grow vegetables than flowers.

Vegetables are very useful. They can be used for the table and are great produce which can be stored to last indefinitely. Think of the pickles and jams that are in the cupboard. Vegetables can also be used to feed stock and other animals which help with the feed bills. They are a very useful thing to grow. Flowers on the other hand are pretty but also pretty useless. They are handy only for looking at. Surely then you can see that vegetables are better to grow.

Vegetables can also be used for many things. If you want some flowers they have them. If you want food vegetables certainly fit the bill. If you want to make craft items turn to vegetables like gourds and pumpkins. Vegetables are also used in companion plantings to stop pests. They are also used in medicines and cures. Vegetables are the all-purpose plant unlike flowers which can only be admired and that is only for a short time.

People will always want food like vegetables in hard times and they can be used for income or trade for other items. Flowers are the last thing on people's minds when they are struggling to survive.

Overall vegetables are far better to grow than flowers for the reasons outlined.

6. Schools should make lunchtime longer

Schools should not make lunchtime longer as students already have too much free time and should be focused on learning not amusement. Let's face it school is only six hours a day and that is constantly interrupted by recess and lunch as it is. Students need more time in class not more time in the playground. It is a terrible idea to make lunchtime longer and there are no good reasons for it.

When at school students need to be focused on learning not amusement. A long lunchtime would be detrimental to this as students would be focused even more on their breaks rather than on their work. An extended lunchtime would be a waste of time. Students just need to time to eat lunch and then go to the toilet before heading into class for some serious learning.

School is only open for a short time and each minute should be used well. If lunchtime is extended when you add in recess over twenty percent of the day could be lost. This is a very bad thing for learning and isn't what school is about? We need to use every valuable minute to extend our minds rather than our legs. Let's keep our kids in the classroom not in the playground.

The interruptions to learning that are recess and lunchtime should be kept to a minimum to get the maximum benefit from students' short time at school. Don't even mention the ten week's holiday each year that interrupts quality education. If we are realistic about learning we cannot extend lunchtime any more. It is long enough now.

Schools should not, under any circumstance, make lunchtimes longer.

7. Persuade an adult to buy something you really want

The thing that I want and need the most is a new computer. A second hand computer is not good enough these days when speed is so important. A computer is also invaluable for school and general educational purposes. Finally a computer is also a fabulous asset for social communication and relaxation. A computer is the best all-purpose tool a person could have.

If I had a new computer everything would be done so much quicker and valuable time would not be wasted. I would not have to spend so much time on it and would be able to do other things like help around the house and yard. My current computer does not allow me to do much and it is very slow. Many of my school activities cannot proceed because of its age.

This raises another vital reason why I need a new computer. Without a computer it is nearly impossible to get a solid education in these modern times. Every piece of school work is completed on computer and this is also how most research is now conducted. This is the main reason for getting me a new computer, the educational benefits. I want to be able to achieve at the highest level and this new computer will enable me to do that.

A smaller but significant benefit is the social aspect of the new computer you're getting me. Instead of expesive phone calls I can contact my friends for free in real time. I can also play games which will stop me bothering you when I'm bored.

I'm sure these excellent reasons are enough to convince you I really need that new computer.

Sample Responses - Descriptive Writing

8. Garden

My garden is large enough for us to have plenty of grassy space to play hide and seek, soccer and cricket. My mother and father have lots of flower gardens which they spend time in each weekend while my sister and two brothers play.

The gardens are filled with flowers of every imaginable colour. In spring you can see the blues, reds, yellows, pinks and whites from the road. People who walk past tell my parents they can smell the fragrance from the different plants as you walk past. The flowers are in many shapes and sizes but my favourites are the purple pansies and the bright blue cornflowers.

The front garden also has a hedge to stop people seeing in all the way. The plant in the hedge is called plumbago and it has blue and white flowers and is always green even in winter. This hedge is clipped back with big cutters each year or else it would get too high. Dad says it needs to be kept tidy and under control.

My favourite place in the garden is the old mulberry tree in the backyard. It is about ten times taller than me and the thick, brown branches are good for climbing. The leaves are soft so they don't scratch you and each year it has fruit on it which are purple and taste delicious. The mulberry juice stains your teeth and tongue. Sometimes it even stains your clothes.

My garden is a safe and pleasant place to play and on Sundays we might have a barbecue for lunch and sit at the outside table to eat. That's always fun.

9. Game

I love playing Blockus because it's a game of strategy where you can play and beat the rest of your family. In my family the four of us play the game and sometimes I can beat both my parents and my older sister. I started playing the game when I was five which is the earliest you can play the game.

There are four colours on the board which are red, yellow, green and blue. I like blue and always choose it if I can. You get twenty-one pieces to start and you have to start from the corner of the playing board. All the pieces are different shapes and it gets complicated the further you go.

You can only put your pieces on the corner of another of your pieces and they cannot be in contact along an edge of the same colour. It doesn't matter much about touching the other colours but with all those pieces the board gets very crowded with all the coloured pieces. The board looks like a rainbow at the end.

You have to get all or as many pieces as you can on the board. If you get all your pieces on without being blocked by another colour you win. If nobody can move the winner is decided by the person with the least pieces left. Sometimes we argue about different moves and sometimes Kayte, my sister, tries to cheat just to beat me.

Blockus is a very exciting and challenging game to play. You need to concentrate very hard to win. That's why I like it.

10. Horses

The mare walked smoothly around the yard. Her four strong legs looked like they could carry her great distances and her hooves stirred up puffs of dust as she walked. She flicked her head as the pace of her walk increased to a trot. This mare looked ready to run but she was kept in check by the wooden rails of the horse yard.

I had chosen this mare to ride because of her long, well developed back, good training and excellent temperament. The owner told me she was a very well mannered horse and easily trained. She came toward me and I could see into her large brown eyes that she was kind. As I held out the carrot for her she pushed out her long pink tongue and gently took the treat from my steady hand.

Now up close I could smell her horsey odour and reached out automatically to pat her neck. She arched and stayed steady as I touched her warm hair and gave her a big pat with my open hand. She seemed to like this and edged closer to the rail. Right then I decided to call her Amilee after my grandmother whom I loved very much.

I kept my hand on her neck and talked to her. I could see her ears prick up as I talked and knew she was listening to me. I was so happy that I had bought this grey mare with her spotted colouring. Amille neighed loudly and sprang to life as she trotted around the yard showing off. I decided then and there to walk back to the tack shed and get a bridle and saddle.

It was definitely time to ride my horse.

Sample Responses - Recounts

11. Best Birthday

My best birthday was the birthday party I had when I was eight. It had everything that a fantastic birthday should have; friends, family, presents and a wonderful time. Let me tell you about it.

When I woke up in the morning we had a family gathering and I received the presents my family had bought me. I had a new computer, an MP3 player, and some games for the Playstation and clothing. What a fabulous start to the day. Then mum made pancakes for breakfast which we all enjoyed thoroughly.

We then got ready and went to my grandparent's place where we had morning tea. They gave me some games for the new computer which was really nice of them. On the way home mum and dad bought all the things we needed for the afternoon. I got to choose the foods that my friends and I would eat.

At three o'clock my three best friends came over and to top it off a big truck arrived with a jumping castle. We stayed on it all afternoon long before becoming very tired of jumping. As it was a sleepover my friends stayed for tea and we ate pizza and all the yummy lollies we bought earlier in the day.

My friends and I stayed up very late and watched a scary movie. We then stayed in our sleeping bags and talked and told jokes until nearly midnight. We soon fell asleep because we were so tired. We woke the next morning very early and continued to talk. My friends had a great time. What a birthday!

12. Worst Holiday

My worst holiday ever was the year we went to Fiji and got caught in a tropical cyclone. The holiday began well enough with an easy trip to the airport and a sweet, smooth flight over the ocean and into the capital of Fiji, Suva. Even the short helicopter ride out to the islands was very enjoyable as always.

The trouble only began after a week on our island resort. That first week was brilliant, great snorkelling, wonderful food and superb fishing. Unfortunately on that final Friday things began to turn nasty. We awoke to a leaden sky with winds that buffeted us while eating breakfast. The locals told us there was a storm warning but nobody seemed to have any idea it would develop into a full blown cyclone.

We planned to continue for the final three days and just work around the storm which would blow out. Well that didn't happen. We ended up on the island resort for another week, spending most of that time in the shelter of the main building. We even slept there for safety as some of the cabanas had their roofs blown off by the heavy winds. I have never seen so much rain come down and hope to never see it again. Everything and everywhere was wet.

Finally the cyclone subsided somewhat and we could get a ferry back to the mainland. Even then it was three days before any flights left the airport. We were late home and exhausted. If we were looking for adventure on that holiday we got it but we weren't. It was supposed to be a wind down from a hectic year.

Never mind there's always next year's holiday!

13. Accident

The worst accident I have ever seen was when my little brother, Jessie, fell out of the Chinese Elm we used to climb in the front yard. It was a great place for us to play in the afternoons and you could climb up and watch all the surrounding houses without being seen. Amazingly it was one of the few big trees left in our suburb and it was in our yard.

Anyway the accident happened one afternoon. We had come home from school and ripped into a great afternoon tea as you do. We had bundled it all up and had some drinks as well to take up the tree. Jessie waited at the bottom of the tree to pass the stuff up and I would take it while he climbed. We used to sit on the higher branches and eat to get a better view.

Unfortunately that day Jessie climbed past me and sat on the branch as usual but when I passed him the food he must have overbalanced. He fell down through the tree bouncing off some quite large branches. You could hear the thud as he hit the ground and I was very worried as he was quiet. I climbed down and called out to mum very loudly.

Mum came flying out of the house and rushed over to Jessie. He was not unconscious but looked pretty badly shaken. Mum left me with him and rushed to ring an ambulance which came very quickly. He went to hospital but really all he had was a broken arm and lots of bruises. The ambulance man said it was mostly shock.

Still it was the worst accident I had ever seen.

Sample Responses - Information Reports

14. Dinosaurs

What are dinosaurs?

Dinosaurs were a large group of very different animals many millions of years ago. They are mainly reptiles and birds with more than one thousand five hundred species. The word dinosaur was given by a British scientist Richard Owen and it means 'terrible, powerful, wondrous lizard'.

What did dinosaurs eat?

Dinosaurs ate both plants and animals. This means some were carnivores(meat eating) and some were herbivores (plant eating). Some dinosaurs ate both plants and animals which means they were omnivores.

What happened to the dinosaurs?

There are no true dinosaurs left on earth and they became extinct. Other types of animals on earth also became extinct at this time and scientists think a meteor hit the earth and changed the atmosphere. There are some other theories about the extinction and one is that the dinosaurs just failed to adapt to a changing world environment.

How do we know about dinosaurs?

We know about dinosaurs through fossils of dinosaur bones that scientists have dug up from the ground. They find bones and then reassemble them to show what the animal looked like. You can see dinosaur bones in museums.

15. Scooters

What are scooters?

Scooters come in all types and you may be surprised what a scooter is. They range from the well known kick scooter that you push yourself to the two wheeled motor driven varieties that are commonly called motor scooters. There are about ten different types of scooter.

The kick scooter

The kick scooter is the most common form of scooter in the world. In olden days these scooters had large soft wheels with a solid metal frame that did not fold. They were a huge children's favourite for decades. More recently the foldable aluminium scooter with hard wheels has become popular as you can perform tricks on them. These are the kind you see at skate parks.

The motor scooter

Motor scooters have a step through frame and they are very convenient in cities for personal transport. They are cheap to buy and run because they are smaller than a motorbike with engines from 50cc to 250cc. They are easy to park and cheap to insure. Many people favour them as a means of transport. Scooter like this can be seen in all big cities and common types are the Vespa and the Lambretta.

16. Bread

Types of bread

There are many different types of bread depending on what ingredients are used. The most common is white bread made from wheat-flour but bread can also be made from rye, barley, maize and oats. On the supermarket shelf you might see types like white, wholemeal, wholegrain, rye, unleavened bread and sourdough.

How bread is made

Bread is made from flour, water, yeast and/or baking soda. Other ingredients can be put in the mix such as milk, eggs, sugar, fruit, vegetables and seeds. Bread is made many different ways around the world.

How bread is cooked

Bread can be cooked in any number of ways but the most common is baking in an oven. It can also be steamed and fried. Most bread in Australia is baked in large ovens.

Why is bread important?

Bread is a very important food and was one of the first foods ever made. It dates back to early man and Neolithic times. Most people eat bread sometime through the day and it is regarded as a staple and fresh bread is still a highly regarded food. It is kept fresh in plastic wrap to stop it drying out.

Sample Responses - Narrative Writing

17 Treasure

The desert was so hot. The sand went on forever and each step was very difficult. I didn't think that my friends and I would make it out alive. We had been lost when our little plane crashed on our way to my parents' worksite at the pyramids. The pilot was injured badly so we went for help. So far we'd found nothing and Sally looked very sunburnt and tired. Nathaniel was dragging his leg which had been wrenched in the crash.

I didn't feel all that well myself and with the water running out things were not looking positive. If we didn't find someone or something soon we would not be able to save ourselves, let alone the pilot. I adjusted my hat and pushed ahead.

'I think were not gonna make it,' said Nathaniel. 'It is too hot to survive out here.'

'Be positive,' I replied smiling at Sally. 'We'll be fine we just have to keep going.'

The three of us continued to walk in silence. Sand dune after sand dune we climbed. I was beginning to feel that we were in big trouble when in the distance I saw what looked like an oasis. I shouted with joy but Sally warned it might be a mirage.

We ran toward it and it was real! Inside the shade of the palm trees was a small well made by the local tribesmen. The water inside was better than any treasure we could have found. Refreshed and cool we knew someone would come here soon and we were saved.

18. Lost

Each day that passed made finding it more difficult. Everyone was upset, especially mum. After all it was her wedding ring and the most valuable possession she had except for us kids. She had lost it last Tuesday somewhere on the way to or out in the paddock when she was feeding the horses. Since then we had been looking for it all over the place.

'Think carefully,' Dad said for the millionth time. 'Where did you walk. We just have to retrace your steps. Then we'll find it for sure.'

Mum just burst into tears again and Dad looked even more frustrated. We were all saddened by the loss but knew we'd have to be lucky to find it out there in thirty acres of paddock.

Changing the subject I said, 'I'm going to look around the feed bays. The horses may have stood on it. It may be covered it in dust or feed.'

Jemma followed me out not wanting to stay in the dismal kitchen. Things weren't going to get better until the ring was found. That was for sure. We headed through the gate and swung around to the feed area. It was only a short walk to the paddock and it had been scoured carefully over the past days.

I hoisted Gemma over the fence and we began to look again. We had to find it soon so life could get back to normal. I'm sure it will turn up but I do hope it's today!

19. Island

I had never seen an island before and didn't really want to now. My ship, The Albatross, had been swept ashore by a typical Caribbean storm and I just wanted to be gone. The men were organising repairs on the beach while others went inland for resources.

It was my third trip to the area and the first trouble I'd met as Captain. Each trip back to England had been more profitable and now our cargo of sugar and molasses had to be unloaded and repacked before we could sail. It was a real nuisance but nothing could be done.

The island itself wasn't a bad place to be forced onto. At least the beach was sandy, not rocky, and the ship was only slightly damaged. There were some supplies like water, fruits and coconuts and no signs of life such as huts or people. It was deserted which made it safe. The men seemed to enjoy being on land and having fresh food and water. Some even fished off the beach during their evenings.

Turning I saw a team of men return with the wood we needed. Large logs that they would turn to the planks we needed. It was hot work in the tropical sun and I went to give them encouragement for a job well done. I told them all that it was extra rations tonight and they cheered loudly.

It seemed now we could get on with the job and get off the island. After all we weren't on holidays but had a job to do. We were sailors after all not tourists.